See where the man wakes late from his dreaming,
    Late in the night from the sleep that has been;
See where regret weeps sick for the seeming,
    See where the soul shrinks chill from the seen:
The full warm visions that promised to ease him,
    That held for some dream-sake his heart in a chain,
These have rolled from his waking, to chasten and please him
Never again.

II

The man wakes late from the dream of his youth-time,
    Wakes him to know that he knows he is man;
Wakes in the dark of a fathomless truth-time,
    Clutched by the cold of a cosmical plan;
Sure it is only the glamour that's going,
    Sure that the dark has been there from the first;
Nothing has changed save his dream into knowing,
Sure of the worst.

III

Ever the cold of the night all about him
    Mocks at his passionate prayer to prevail;
Ever the silence of world-work without him
    Leaves him permission to conquer or fail:
Fail for the sake of the fervour of loving,
    Conquer for name of the love of the right;
Never a god-glance to mark the approving,
Only the night.

IV

Oh, for the warmth of the sun in a vision!
    Oh, for the vision of suns out of view!
Oh, for the pledge that the infinite prison
    Where bound are the suns, there may be spirits break through!
High in the north of the sky, ever steady,
    A pole-star stands in the whirl of the dark,
A sun hung far at waste and unready,
Less than a spark.

V

Poems, Lyrics, & Sonnets by Louisa Sarah Bevington

Louisa Sarah Bevington was born at St John's Hill, Battersea on 14th May 1845, the eldest of eight children to Quaker parents; Alexander, a member of Lloyds, and Lousia.

Details of her early life are scanty although in the census of 1861 she is listed as a scholar at Marlborough House, Winchcombe Street, Cheltenham. At the time her parents and siblings are listed as residing at Walthamstow with their four house servants and a coachman.

Louisa wrote poetry from a young age and she had two sonnets published in October 1871 in the Friends' Quarterly Examiner.

Her first collection, 'Key Notes', a slim volume of only 23 pages, was published under her pseudonym Arbor Leigh in 1876. A second publication, 'Key-Notes: 1879', written under the name L. S. Bevington also took issue with some Christian codes of conduct.

In her article in The Nineteenth Century in October 1879, 'Atheism and Morality', her secular pose provoked a clerical response. In December the same year, Bevington concluded a two-part essay entitled 'Modern Atheism and Mr. Mallock'. This was in response to an attack on atheism in the same paper by a young Oxford graduate. Louisa put forward a spirited defence of secular morality.

Louisa received a letter from the philosopher Herbert Spencer, confirming that rationalists showed greater humanity than adherents of organized religion. Her exposition of this was published in The Fortnightly Review in August 1881 as 'The Moral Colour of Rationalism'.

In 1882 'Poems, Lyrics & Sonnets' contained both metrical experiments as well as remarks on the stagnant state of Christianity. Her politics were coming into focus.

Louisa travelled to Germany in 1883 and on 2nd May she married the artist Ignatz Guggenberger in Munich. She found married life in Germany dull and humdrum. By 1890 the marriage was over and she returned to London.

Here she took to joining anarchist circles and preferred the use of her maiden name. In 1891 she commented to a preference for "L. S. Bevington" over "Miss Bevington", as she objected to the values "Mrs" and "Miss", although she did sign that letter "L. S. Guggenberger".

Louisa quickly gained credence as an anarchist poet and was also helped by her friends Charlotte Wilson and Peter Kropotkin who had founded the anarchist paper Freedom in 1886. Louisa sought distance from advocacy of bombs and dynamite and became associated with another paper, Liberty, edited by the Scottish anarchist and tailor James Tochatti, for which she wrote numerous articles and poems. She was also a contributor to The Torch, which was edited by the Rossetti sisters, nieces of the painter. She also authored the Anarchist Manifesto in 1895 for the short-lived Anarchist Communist Alliance.

Louisa Sarah Bevington died due to dropsy and mitral heart disease on 28th November 1895 at the age of fifty in Willesden Green. She was buried at Finchley Cemetery.

Index of Contents

POEMS AND LYRICS

Low in the east of the sky is a glimmer,
   Dawn or false dawn in a piteous show;
Dimmer the stars are, dimmer and dimmer,
   Why has the dawn not a homelier glow?
Oh, the late night is all pallid and eerie!
   Oh, the old dreams were familiar and kind!
Woe to the man that he wakes him aweary,
Blinder than blind.

VI

Breathes there a sigh from the transient pallor?
   Yearns there a whisper from heaven's new sheen?
Comes there a hope to inspire him to valour
   Echoed from edge of the sleep that has been?
How on the grey fields find him fruition?
   How in the stark frost rouse him to move?
How in the thin white light of perdition
Find him a love?

VII

Fears he a falsity hinting of morning,
   Echoed of genii 'twixt mutter and grin;
Shivers his spirit, and takes for a warning
   Light that is sunless, and hope that is sin.
Shall there be wailing, or shall there be drinking?
   Shall there be mercy, or shall there be hate?
Shall there be eagerness freed from the thinking?
What is the fate?

VIII

See, as he watches, that dawn before dawning
   Streams to wild apex against the high dark;
Faint, whence the starless abysses are yawning,
   Cries the far herald—"Arouse ye, and hark!"
Strained is his soul to the voice of the message,
   New to his ear is the tone of the cry;
Strained is his sight to interpret the presage
There in the sky.

IX

Glimmer there is, but a glimmer that goeth,
    The faint false morning that owns not a sun;
Yet he can see by it; ay, and it showeth
    Far are the sands of the night-time run;
Darkness will swallow the shine for an hour—
    A black last hour ere the true day be—
Lo! the man searches to pluck him a flower
While he can see.

X

Total the pressure no impulse that knoweth,
    Forth from loose elements onward to life,
Stress to be one, that asunder yet throweth,
    Stress to prevail in an infinite strife;
Blind is the wind that brings thistledown hither,
    Numb is the sod where the thistledown roots,
Deaf are the rainfloods that water or wither
Where the plant shoots.

XI

What does the man find, prize of his waking,
    Said by the silence, shown by the dark?
What is the meaning beyond his mistaking?
    What is the mute aim worthy his mark?
Infinite ages through infinite travail
    Have brought him afire and aware and aghast,
And awfully bid him a dream to unravel
Here at the last.

XII

Driven a centre of life into loving,
    Driven through fury of love into sin,
Driven of sin into direst reproving,
    Driven by bitterness sorrow to win;
Atoms must be, if the atoms shall mingle;
    Prosper the unit or prosper the clan?
What is the man's life?—cosmical? single?
Who is the man?

XIII

Claim of a universe simple of tissue
    Ever to break into multiple mind;
Clash of all units to mix and bear issue,
    Jangle of fetters that sunder and bind;
Strong is the stress of the life and the moving,
    One is the blindness and one is the might,
Complex the suffering, scattered the proving,
Diverse the right.

XIV

If there be victory, who shall declare it?
    Victor or vanquished? and what of the claim?
Is there a boon, will he treasure or spare it?
    Shall he fight hardest for love or for fame?
What though the plaint of his heart unavailing
    Deaden to silence of passionate will,
Shall he not firmlier fight for prevailing?
Conqueror still?

XV

Ha! there is light, though it warms but a little;
    Ha! there is morning, though naked and cold;
Waking be welcome, for visions are brittle;
    Patience, ye prophets! ye heroes, be bold!
Lo! the distress, the despair, the aloneness,—
    Fire of blind forces and cold of the soul,—
Till the torn world grope back to its oneness,
Warm with the whole.

THE VALLEY OF REMORSE

There goes a wandering soul in desert places;
(Good Lord, deliver!)
About its way lie dumb, with livid faces,
Slain virtures and slain hopes in locked embraces;
(Good Lord, deliver!)
And drear black crags tower from unholy ground
Sheer upward in thick air,
Where breathes no prayer;
No wind is there,

No sound; (Good Lord, deliver!)
And there is no way out, and round and round,
With haggard eye and dragged and staggering paces,
Through years that soul a ghastly circuit traces.
(Good Lord, deliver!)

The sun, all shorn of rays, with lurid fire
Blasts where it strikes: Doom's own red eye of ire:
And all night long is seen unhallowed shimmer,—
Half life, half mire,—
Of things made manifest that should be hid;
Yet Will is numb that should their play forbid;
And so they crowd and crawl in gloom and glimmer,
Loathed and unchid;
And lo! that soul among them, moving dimmer.
(Good Lord, deliver!)

At the soul's back behold a burden yonder,
A monstrous thing of slime;
Two paces forth,—no more,—that Doomed may wander
For all its time;—
Two wretched paces from the accursèd weight
Bound on by linkèd fate
In glittering cynic chain two steps behind it;
(Good Lord, deliver!)
Such steely bond between
Forbids it breath, save only to remind it,
The Past has been,
The Past of sin. (Good Lord, deliver!)

Ay! just where life if holiest—at the source
Of the soft, ruffled wings,—is chained the curse.
(Good Lord, deliver!)
Those pinions, once all light and wide of feather
That soared right loftily, see, clamped together;
And quivering life is gallèd at the spot,
Sore hurt and hot: (Good Lord, deliver!)
Yet, chafes that soul rebellious at the tether?
Or, in vain swiftness seeks to flee the load?
Then heavier fall the blood-drops on the road:—
(Good Lord, deliver!)

The loathèd burden of unburied death
Flies fast as flies that Doomed, or drags as slow;
(Good Lord, deliver!)
Two paces forward ever it may go;
No more; the burden grimly followeth.
There is no freedom here,

Nor any cheer!   (Good Lord, deliver!)
Not lightened yet to skeleton, nor dried,
The load yields horror, horror yet beside;
Fell fumes, half poison and half sustenance,
That hinder life, and hinder deathly trance.
Is there a chance?   (Good Lord, deliver!)

Three virgin forms came passing by but lately,
Treading the desert boldly and sedately,
Calling it 'beauteous earth';
Who met this Doomed, and gazed upon it straightly;
(Good Lord, deliver!)
These saw no burden, so they praised the chain;
Its teracherous glitter seemed some bauble worn
About the wingèd shoulders to adorn.
(Good Lord, deliver!)

They noted on the path no shocking stain,
So, as the soul made moan,
Knowing no whit of conflict nor of pain,
Deemed it most vain;
And answered in gay tone—
"Now Heaven deliver thee,
Spirit alone!—
Why grievest thou when every bird is singing,
And glad white cloudlets high in ether winging
Brighten e'en sunshine? Hear the steeples ringing
With marriage mirth!
Behold life blest with love and holiday
While thou art stricken, bent, and wan to see;
Good Lord, deliver thee!"

All mutely points that soul beyond the chain
Two paces backward; points in vain, in vain;—
Who sees not, cannot aid.
Oh, kind, unkindly virgin sympathy!
Oh, blind, hell-deepening heavenly mockery!
What though each maid
Had pitied had she seen; not one could see,
Not one of three. (Good Lord, deliver!)

They passed, and music with them. Then there came
Three little children, joying e'en the same,
Yet sweetlier still. They called the desert "May."
(Good Lord, deliver!)
"Come play with us at play;
Blue skies and meadows green are friends to-day;
Spread thy good wings, that we may mount thereon

And seek of all the clouds the whitest one
To tiptoe on its top toward the sun;
And prove whose sight is strongest!
And who can gaze the longest!
Our little eyes are clear,—
Young, but so clear!
In each of thine there trembles half a tear!
Ah! fun!—
We see where thou canst see not; in the eye
Of the great golden sun that crowns the sky!"
(Good Lord, deliver!)

A mother and a father wandered by:
Hand locked in hand.—"This way the children went,"
Quoth he, "on some enchanting mischief bent;
Behold, their little footprints thickly lie."
"Bless them!" quoth she: then closer to his side
Drew shudderingly: "An influence is here,
Here in the air; the sunlight seemeth drear;
Oh lead me hence!" And he:
"'Tis so; I see a form unmeet to see
Advancing painfully.
Oh, fear!
Lest the sweet babies lingered near the spot,
For something foul doth surely somewhere rot;
It boots not to know what.
Hence! spirit dear."
(Good Lord, deliver!)

Maiden and babe and mother have passed by
Scatheless, yet left the doom-glare red and high
Above that blackened valley of all dole,
Nor freed the laden soul.
Crawl, ye foul formless ills! about your prey;
Sink, O thrice lost! forsaken on the way;
Perish from day!
Since thrice hath passed in vain the innocent,
And hope is long, long spent,
And will is rent.
(Good Lord! Great God! deliver! deliver!)

Lo! Love comes wandering on the desert way.
Oh, watch! oh, pray!
Love with the rose-wreath red?
Ay, love rose-bound!
Ay, love thorn-crowned!
Crowned—bound—with cruel rose-thorns round his head!
(Good Lord, deliver!)

Love! love is here! that knoweth of all pain,
And of the linkèd chain,
And of the stain,
And of the whirling madness, dumb and dread;
Love! love is here that knoweth nought in vain!
Dead hope, dead will, oh! cry
Aloud! Love passeth by;
Love, that can love dead life to live again!
(Good Lord, deliver!)

New radiance hallows all the sickened air;
For love is here.
And right and left spring lilies at his nod,
Blessing the blighted sod;
For love is here.
 And round the gaunt crags echo of deep prayer
Is sighing everywhere,—
Is sighing everywhere!
For love is here.
(Deliver! Lord, deliver!)

Kneels that worn soul, for all the place is holy;
Breaks that sore heart, in utterance lost and lowly;
"For Love's dear sake, great Powers, deliver me!
O LOVE, deliver me!"

A little bird sweet twitters in a tree;
A little breeze comes coolly from the sea;
And broad the dawn-light widens o'er the lea.

PENT

Take me to some waste of being,
   Virgin spaces, dark and far,
Seas no vessel ever burdened,
   Skies that never held a star;
There, my inmost soul all weeping,
I may loose for Being's keeping
   Strange, abysmal thoughts that are.

Let me stand, alone, unguarded,
   On some crag where fierce floods beat;
Let hoarse tempest crash and echo,
   Storm-fire lick about my feet;
In the hollow air of thunder

I may shout my soul asunder,
　　One pent syllable repeat.

　Let me sink where waves are deepest,
　　Die from memory and air;
Let effacing billows deafen
　　Question, when I lived, or where;
Only first be mine to murmur
Thrice, and ever fiercely firmer,
　　For I must—one life-pent prayer.

WRESTLING

Our oneness is the wrestlers', fierce and close,
Thrusting and thrust;
One life in dual effort for one prize,—
We fight, and must;
For soul with soul does battle evermore
Till love be trust.

Our distance is love's severance; sense divides,
Each is but each;
Never the very hidden spirit of thee
My life doth reach;
Twain! since we love athwart the gulf that needs
Kisses and speech.

Ah! wrestle closelier! we draw nearer so
Than any bliss
Can bring twain souls who would be whole and one,
Too near to kiss:
To be one thought, one voice before we die,—
Wrestle for this.

BEES IN CLOVER

A SONG

Up the dewy slopes of morning
Follow me;
Every smoky spy-glass scorning,
Look and see, look and see
How the simple sun is rising,
Not approving nor despising

You and me.
Hear not those who bid you wait
Till they find the sun's birth-date,
Preaching children, savage sages,
To their mouldy, blood-stuck pages
And the quarrelling of ages,
Leave them all; and come and see
Just the little honied clover,
 As the winging music-bees
Come in busy twos and threes
Humming over!
All without a theory
Quite successfully, you see;
Little priests that wed the flowers,
Little preachers in their way,
Through the sunny working day
With their quite unconscious powers
How they say their simple say.
    What? a church-bell in the valley?
What? a wife-shriek in the alley?
Tune the bell a little better,
Help the woman bear her fetter.
All in time! all in time!
If you will but take your fill
Of the dawn-light on the hill,
And behold the dew-gems glisten,—
If you turn your soul to listen
To the bees among the thyme,
There may chance a notion to you
To encourage and renew you,
For the doing and the speaking,
Ere the jarring of the chime,
 And the mad despair of shrieking
Call you downward to the mending
Of a folly, and the ending
Of a crime.
    On the dewy hill at morning
Do you ask?—do you ask?
How to tune the bells that jangle?
How to still the hearts that wrangle?—
For a task?
When the bell shall suit the ears
Of the strong man's hopes and fears,
As the bee-wing suits the clover
And the clover suits the bee,
Then the din shall all be over,
And the woman shall be free,
And the bell ring melody,

Do you see?—do you see?
There are bees upon the hill,
And the sun is climbing still,
To his noon;
Shall it not be pretty soon
That the wife she shall be well,
And the jarring of the bell
Falls in tune?

WHITHER?

Through the fathomless peace of the starlight,
    Through the feverish travail of mind,
Through the love of the live heart within me,
    I search,—and this ever I find:

Totality, busy creating,
    Through being, the law that I see;
A universe steadily working
    The work that shall render it free.

When the patience of law universal
    Shall issue in mastery of law,—
When the freedom that grows of the "must be"
    Shall reign in its infinite awe.

When virtue is lost in its issue,
    When sweetly hath blossomed the rod,
The fruit of Totality's travail—
    The ultimate rest—shall be "GOD."

YOUR TREASURE

Long years—you say—you had a quest,
    You sought a blossom fine and sweet
    And perfect, that your soul might greet
To win and cherish as your best.

And once, and more than once, you seemed
    To near it in your wandering,
    Yet only grasped a common thing
That mocked you where you yearned and dreamed.

And as you told me of your grief,

And how you yielded up your hope,
   There laughed through tears on heaven's slope
A little wingèd angel-thief;

Who, as your aspiration went—
   Dead, as you thought—in your spent cry,
   Caught it and held it up on high,
And to my soul a whisper sent:—

"He shall not miss it—strong and meek;
   Though scarcely on the soil of earth
   Spring his fine treasure into birth,
Yet may you find it if you seek.

And having won it, bear it home
   To where his heart still craveth it,
   Where, though in desolation's pit,
His will and spirit yet o'ercome."

Then softened in me all my strife,
   Then seemed my chains to set me free,
   Then, dear, there dawned in peace to me
The first clear morning of my life.

What once you sought, behold I found,—
   The rare, strange blossom, passing sweet;
   For when I bowed me at your feet
I saw it where they met the ground.

And as you moved your soul away
   I reached my hand and grasped the flower,
   And from that saddest, holiest hour
Here in my bosom doth it stay.

And here I hold it till you turn,
   And by its perfume know its face;—
   Till having gazed a little space
Its finding you may care to learn.

Of how, because you longed for it,
   And it was worthy to be born,
   It sprang on that same tearful morn
Close in the shadow of your feet.

And how, because my head was low
   For my most deep repentance' sake,
   I, all unworthy, saw it wake,
I, even I, beheld it grow.

And how, as since, the days have run,—
    Repentant days that teach like years,
    In floods of ruthful, tender tears
I've watered it,—the dearly-won!

And how some hearts that caught its scent—
    Hearts very weak and very pressed—
    Took courage, and with hope possessed,
Smiled the more sweetly as they went.

Ay, how one came in soiled despair
    And saw the radiance of your flower,
    And felt the pureness of its power,
And woke to aspiration fair.

'Tis starnge that I, whose heart, earth-bound,
    Believed not in it,—for my fate
    Should find and prize it even late,
While you who sought it, never found.

'Tis sweet that loving made the way
    To penitence, so weeping laid
    My whole soul meekly in the shade
Where your dear doubted treasure lay.

Your eyes were sunward as you sought;
    What recks the eagle where his wings
    Screens from the sun-fire weaker things?
'Twas so your searching came to nought.

You could not see it, reason clear;
    'Tis I must nurture hour by hour
    That pure, sweet, half-unearthly flower
That sprang in your own shadow, dear.

And if—and when—you turn and see,
    It may be you'll forget the past,
    And smile, and own your crown at last,—
Your holy, high love victory.

THE PESSIMIST

I wandered yesternight 'twixt sleep and sleep
On the wild outmost coast of consciousness,
Where beat forever waves of paradox,

Fringing abysmal seas of formless fact
That baffle order and omnipotence;
There man finds never thought; and God, no utterance.

In vision I beheld the perfect man
Stand, with all victory behind his back,
Facing the Vague that shapes the shores of sense,
The firm Unfelt, that rims the realm of mind.
Unemphasisèd rhythms of all worlds,
And unimpassioned ceaselessness of years
Mocked him, and penetrated, where he stood
Knowing all knowledge, comprehending life,
Brought to the final equilibriate bound
That is quiescence. There he pardoned God.
 He pardoned, for he pitied. He had passed
Perilously through passion into pain,
Passionately through pain to numb despair;
In diverse fulness of his spirit's strength,
Had trode the devious ways of human lot
From first to latest, proving one by one
Those four weird worlds each prophet traverses—
Four phases of the deep, mad mystery
Men lightly nickname "Life,"—four mystic spheres
Where-through wills work a purpose not their own.

    Eden, whose innocence nor sinks nor soars,
Nor knows it doth not either, nor can know
Because of innocence; where words afloat,
Intruding from without, lose in calm air
All import, keeping syllables to aid
Pale souls to speak pale trifles; where the sun
Shines with a tempered heat, a safe, white light
That nothing blasts, and nothing finely fires.
Here in the unfelt peace of flower-life
Move the Untried on level, middling ways;
Harmless and unimpeded: unaware
Of Eden's Eden-hood. He had been there.

    Then conflict-plain of that mid wilderness
Outside the Eden-gate, where sense and soul
Strive in perplexèd writhings of wrought life,
Half base, half glorious; bringing conscience forth
As victor, or as scourge. He had been there.

    Blood drives: light beckons. So Gehenna next
Gapes at the urgent feet: fell precipice
Of lawless pit that mocketh liberty,
Where ill flares luridly and inwardly,

Triumphing and despairing; loose, yet gagged,
Lest it spit forth tempestuous taunt to vex
Or wreck the universal hope of souls,
In direst deluge of gall-bitter flame.
There conscience, with some tone of ghastly gibe,
Most impotently riots amid the thoughts
In the soul's worst estate; and reason sways,
Lit and afire with lust. He had been there.

And last, the heaven of high deliverance;—
The love-light that none living entereth.
Yet—haggard with the wanton strife of earth,
And scorched and scarred with the pent woe of hell—
Lost poet souls creep to the verges of,
And peering through its gates, so long to win
That thought lies down in prayer with folded wings,
Or entering dies, the drowned death-joy of love!—
Loosed timelessly from life's own limit-load;—
For the eternal moment one with God.

So had he travelled all the ways of men,
And reached that fringèd coast of formlessness.
The keys were his of prophecy and art,
Flung to him from high heaven to clank in hell,
And unlock all the silences of earth.
But of the sad, sweet, fain philosophies
E'en this was known unto the utmost man,—
True knowledge and its goal are set as foes;
The prize life's agony is borne to win,
Itself the deep, great stillness of spent life,—
The soul-cry spent in crying that ends the strife.

Thus having journeyed, lo! he stood at length
Crying on truth with all his parting strength;
And eloquent in dumbness at his feet
The waves of paradox kept equal beat:—
    "The price of sight is to be blind through light;
    The price of wisdom, value of its veil;
    The price of goodness, innocency's pyre;
    The price of rest, the weariness that slays."
So thundered on his thought's supremest rim
Twin-facts, twin-toned; each mocking each, and him.
Then as the universal darkened down,
And the Unformed swept nearer him, to drown
In all unmeaning ending fate's long frown,—
Then, when his hope's last final flicker waned,
There burst the truth upon:—God is chained!

The unfathomable weariness of God
Bound by his boundlessness to be and be,
Alone and unexpressed, immortally,—
The cause that can effect not, endlessly,—
Fired this last prophet. High he flung his arms
Standing on thought's last verge, and sent his cry
Winged with a soul-sore yearning into space,
Gazing as though his gaze met the mute face
Of God's despair most straightly, eye to eye,
As lovers when they love entirely.
　　And with the outer darkness o'er his head,
And with the dust of death about his feet,
　And with the wreck of hope behind his back,
And with the blank Unthought before his face,
He cried to God a dreadful, final cry,
That was not praise, nor prayer, but—sympathy.

　　"Great Sufferer! God! Helpless Omnipotence!
　That broke thy being into discord dire,
　　To feel thyself alive in chaos-fire
And action, interacting and intense;—
Not thine the curse that life began to be,
To look upon thy misery and thee.

　　We, who are born of thine immense distress,
Being less, and being many, suffer less,
And so may pardon that terrific sigh
That broke from dull deep of thy unity
To wake the clash of forces and our life,
And all the quivering detail of world-strife.

And lo! the riddle of the universe,—
　All this most horrible august mischance
　Of woe-worn being at its grim death-dance,—
Unveiled,—forgiven. God! it had been worse
That thy most awful bosom had not rent
Itself in sob that built the firmament,
And woke the hurrying worlds to ease thy woe,
And life to speak thee to thee, blind and slow.

　　What place for joying while thou art alone?—
Till thou hast known thyself a little known
Let nothing curse thee! Though a myriad fail
Their loss is thine, and may thy life avail;
The pain-born universe is thine own pain
That, till through love it help thee, toils in vain.

　　Be thy grief partly easier, that we weep;

Thy wearying partly easier that we sleep;
Be thy void love the richer that we find
Life not ourselves to love, and kinships kind:
If in our being thine may find relief,
Take thou our love for all our life and grief.

   Ineffable! Eternal! Unexpressed!
Be answer waked where the void deep was mute
Of thine abysmal life. O Absolute!
Take all thou canst of us, so thou may'st rest;
 Help us to help unbind and set thee free,
For Godhead's awful grief take thou man's sympathy."

   The angels looked upon that utmost man
And struck a new wild chord on heavenly harps,
And sang a riven, startled measure forth
To dubious tune of most unheavenly fear.
Psalm, sickened through with satire unaware,
Rang in the doom-struck halls of deity:
"King! thou hast brought forth as the fruit of all
A devil-life to mock thee! Thou art God!"
   The wrecked ones in torture of pent pride
Sneered up from hell-fire: "Ha! consummate birth
Of all time's travail! Trifler with sweet ill
That timely spewed it forth for bitter good!
Hell reads thine inmost heart! Thou finished saint!
So holy grown that thou would'st ransom God,
And die his saviour! So thou did'st aspire
Till there grew from thee rainbow-plumes to soar
To that last wistfulness at heaven's gate,
And found it barred against thee? Grievous saint!
 What hast thou won? What profit, lordly soul?
To tell thy deity he reigns absolved
For damning thee? Why, so absolved are we;
Sure God, man-pardoned, pardons devils that know
So well his pardoner? Whole man! mere man!
Crown of the universe! Most perfect man!"
   The sons of earth beheld him stand and cry
And crave, and pity God, and sympathise,
And speak as one who grasped the utmost end
Of earth's unended conflict; and they said
With shuddering: "Lo! the fruit of genius;
He speaketh with assurance. He is mad!"
   Yet Eden-souls smiled on, nor recked of aught
But that the sun rose, and at evening set.
"See, birds build nests in spring-time; while the moon
And stars light up the garden of the nights,
And rainfall helps the lilies open out,—

The thornless, pallid lilies all about.
    Speak ye of din outside the Eden-gate?
We know of it: the wind is loud at times.
God reigns for all; that outer wilderness—
Dim, hearsay waste—it howls in vain for us:—
 See the white petals curl them thus and thus.
God reigns; blow what wind may through emptiness."

    In vain! O travail of the universe!
In vain! O truth whose depth is in a curse!
There needs no better where there weeps no worse.
For all that he had suffered and had been,
Here, where the Unbegun reposed serene,
Here, where no blended light of ill and good
Inflamed or fired the fencèd sisterhood,—
Not pitied, curst, nor praised, but blankly seen,
The Perfected a bootless, voiceless cypher stood.

STEEL OR GOLD?

THE QUESTION

    Will you have me gold or steel,
   Love, whose crucible is here?
Will you have me brave, or feel
Fate's anguish, dear?
    Am I virtuous—who knows?
   If I glitter in the fire
Harder, whiter, as it glows
At your desire?
    Or yet worthier if I quail
   As the dark dross melts again
If I sometimes nearly fail
For very pain?
    While the steel is growing white
   It grows harder, whiteness near:
While the gold is growing bright
It softens, dear.
    Say then, will you have forth cast,
   When the tale of fire is told,
From your crucible at last
Fine steel, or gold?

GOLD AND STEEL

THE ANSWER

I have asked, and you have answered:—
  Be the cunning work fulfilled,
Be the soul that's tried by fire
  Tender-hearted, warrior-willed.
   Steel for strength and gold for beauty,
  So shall be the heart you hold;
As a sword of keenest metal
  Yet may have its hilt of gold.
   Fan your furnace, hotter, hotter,
  Till you win the weapon true;
Golden to your touch, my dearest,
  Steel, to meet you foes for you.

TILL THE MIST PASSES

Till the mist passes, and ye can descry
  Why hearts for ages loved the love-shed blood
  Of a pure Christ, and praised a humble God,
Hush, ye song-gifted! lest ye sing a lie.

Till the din ceases, and again ye hear
  Echo in your own soul, each one of you,
  Of all that won men to be sad and true,
Wait; that your note through waiting may grow clear.

Swift blisses of a wanton, will-less hour,—
  Soft hair, youth's happy lips, love's laughter low,
  Pall if ye praise nought else; perennial glow
Streams from no age that hymns but half its power.

Men of the morrow! ye of kindliest scan!
  Chaunt still most sweetly what most strength may save,
  Find song for what is difficult and brave,—
For what begins not lowlier than at man.

But ever in its great simplicity
  Supposes all the powers of his blood,
  His strange self-ordering sense of brotherhood,
And all the subtle joys of sympathy.

Fine flavours of discriminated good
  Learnt from the tasting of the knowledge-tree,
  Things that it takes the whole of man to be,

And poets' travail to make understood.

From out the strife of mad, conflicting needs
   So shall your music strike a harmony,
   And hold aloft a meaning steadfastly
Above the ruin-crash of falling creeds.

Be true to man, our poets! Ay, be true
   To both the moods of this twain-natured thing;—
   His breath of self sing if ye will, but sing
Also the utmost man that lives in you.

THE POET'S TEAR

A tear welled up from a poet heart
And fell on a rose;
Lay there, bitter, and made it smart,—
The red, red rose!
Oh, the grief that wept it was full and pent,
And the sobbing pain-blood came and went
As song arose!
When the tear shall dry then shall song be spent;
O tear, lie still in thy bloomy tent,
And cherish thy pain in petal and scent,
Red, tear-filled rose.

The tear-drop hides in the rose's breast
For fear of a ray,—
For fear it should rise in the sun-lit air
And perish of glory and gladness there;—
O worst! O best!
So it quivers to music from day to day,
Hidden in scent and crimson away,
For fear of a ray in a rosy nest;—
O curst! O blest!
Shall the rose smile up in the eager sky
That the sun may give?
Or, shall grief be hidden, and passion shy,
That a song may live?
When the petals yield, then the tear shall dry;
If the heart be healed, so its song shall die;
As the poet grieves, so his music grows;—
O tear! O rose!
Shall song be sweet? or shall love be dear?
O tear-filled rose! and O poet's tear!
Who knows? Who knows?

CLOUD-CLIMBING

Be not discouraged, loved and struggling soul!
   The light is hazy, and the way is cold;
   Yet warmth shall come with climbing; and behold,
There shall be light transcendent at the goal.

Be not discouraged! though a hundred times
   Your foot has slipt upon the upward way;
   The clouds of life are rounded toward the day,
And he is nearest heaven who longest climbs.

Be not discouraged! I am grown one prayer
   That courage never fail you; lest the mist
   And gust of circumstance should, wreathing, twist
Your slackened foothold from the aspiring stair.

You shall not fail! Where billowed cloud is spread,
   Your strenuous aspiration has my will
   To second its intent, until—until
I see you vanish from me overhead.

I would have followed for your very sake,
   But all my strength was spent to help you, dear;
   And when your victory is safe and clear,
I almost think my heart of hearts will break.

O YE JOYS!

O YE joys that none have chanced on!
   O ye goals that none have sought!
O ye gulfs of vacant ether
   Where no starshine has been wrought!—
Do ye hold the chance among you
   Of a perfect, perfect thought?

Of a thought that is a meaning
   For the worlds and all their ways,
For the dawning and the dying
   Of the dumb and actual days,
For the listless depth of doing
   That yet ceases not, nor stays?

Will a harvest e'er be gathered
   Out of forces all broadcast?
Does there lie in any future
   The redemption of a past?
Can the kernel of existence
   Show its worthiness at last?

O Unsought! Unseen! Undreamt of!
   Hold your secret as ye may,
Men are here upon the earth-ball
   With a will to find their way,
And there comes to will fulfilment,
   Though the total word be "Nay."

There shall be a meek defiance
   In the teeth of mystery hurled;
There shall be a human purpose
   Fitly to the morrow curled;
Though the heat and cold of ages
   Wipe the man print off the world;

Ere he vanish he will please him
   With the earth he walks upon;
Ere he perish he will ease him
   Of the dread of living done;
Ere the final fate engulf him,
   All his victory shall be won.

O ye joys that none have chanced on!
   O ye goals that none have sought!
Is there not a hope among you
   Of an all-consoling thought?
Shall not man create a saneness
   Who was bred for blankest nought?

See, the trees succeed a little
   If success be juicy fruit,
And not always has the lily
   E'en a canker at the root;
The sport of fate is kind anon,
   And then the chances shoot.

And how, when chances grown aware
   Have woven them to will,
To find the garden corner
   Where the wind is seldom chill,
To long for fruit, to love the flower,
   To know, and then to till.

Ay, how? When helplessness is death,
   And love is all of bliss,
Shall not the will-work of the world
   Wrench round some fates remiss?
And where the iron whole yields not,
   Yield first, to win a kiss?

"EGOISME À DEUX"

When the great universe hung nebulous
   Betwixt the unprevented and the need,
Was it foreseen that you and I should be?—
Was it decreed?
   While time leaned onward through eternities,
   Unrippled by a breath and undistraught,
Lay there at leisure Will that we should breathe?—
Waited a Thought?
   When the warm swirl of chaos-elements
   Fashioned the chance that woke to sentient strife,
Did there a Longing seek, and hasten on
Our mutual life?
   That flux of many accidents but now
   That brought you near and linked your hand in mine,—
That fused our souls in love's most final faith,—
Was it divine?

VALUATION

Who shall tell the song its value:
   Critic ear, or heart of friend?
Who shall weigh your love's completeness?
   Who shall test the gold you spend?

Not to critic take your poem,
   Not to mintsman take your gold,
Not to idol take your worship,
   If its worth you would be told.

Sing your music to the singer
   Would you be entirely heard;
So your little tune be worthy,
   He will know it; take his word.

Show your coin to any miser

If its metal you would prove;
Ask the heart of any lover,
   He will tell you if you love.

Once the question was to know
Why you came, and why would go,
Once it seem to import so
That I should approve you;
Ay, in lost days dead and dear,
When so often you were here,
I could hope and I could fear;
Now I only love you.

Since your hand hath closed the door,
In my soul for evermore
All is stiller than before;
And the end—who knoweth?
You have gone; to spend your breath,
Haply, on the fields of death
Where the war-fire thundereth
And the palm-tree groweth.

Waves and fates have rolled between,
Things are not that once have been,
Changed the actors, changed the scene
Where the singer stayeth;
If her love hath wrought her woe,
E'en to you, who only know
That it ever hath been so,
Only song betrayeth.

THREE

What of our time?
   (Oracle.)
   A fog and a blur,
A hum and a whirr,
And large mellow lights that are slowly dawning;
Lo! elements mixed,
Lo! centres unfixed,
A hope, and a fear; a chance, and a warning.

What of our time?
  (Pessimist.)
The reign of the worse,
The breath of a curse,
Ash-fruit of man's pride and the knowledge he stole
False witness and fell,
Swift sliding to hell,
The shudder of heaven and the glare of the goal.

What of our time?
  (Optimist.)
The reign of the best
By sympathy's test;
The travail of ages repaid in an age;
The finding of law
Where no prophet foresaw;
Glad glance of man's eye on his destiny's page.

What is our time?
  (Oracle.)
A question of "When?"
An echoed "Amen,"
Vague answering around and below and above;
The hour of the sure,
Yet the hour of the pure,
And a blank new seal on the title of love.

What is our time?
  (Pessimist.)
The death-hour of art;
The rending apart
Of the truth of man's thought from the hope of his life.
The cloud of death-dust
From a pageant of lust,
The triumph of force, and the mocking of strife.

What is our time?
  (Optimist.)
The birth-hour of man,
The dawn of his plan
Whose purpose is life, yet whose cradle a grave;
The time of bold truth,
And of counsel for youth,
And a sword given into the hand of the brave.

What of our time?
  (Oracle.)
Lo! the present re-cast

In the fire of the past
And the future is his who will venture the flame;
Thou child of the hour,
Thy will is its power,
Go claim it, and guide it, and give it thy name.

What is our time?
(Pessimist.)
The great sneer of God
At his animate clod
The oneness of angel, and poet, and beast;
The quenching of prayer
In the lull of despair,
The moan of the woman, the whine of the priest.

What is our time?
(Optimist.)
A greeting of bands,
A meeting of hands,
And barriers broken that hindered the deed;
The idol thrown low
That the Loving may grow
Where the shadow lay dark and the victims yet bleed.

What of the time?
(Oracle.)
Not yet have ye read,
Not yet have ye said,
It is less than your word, it is more than your thought;
Not good and not ill,
But eternal and still;—
What it was; what it shall be; unfound,—and unsought.

UNPERFECTED

Fear hath torment. Love, away!
I'm afraid of you to-day.

Love, your voice I dare not hear,
'Tis so infinitely dear.

Love, I do not dare to see
In your eyes your need of me.

Take to-day your banishment,
Lest I utterly repent.

My weak heart I scarcely know,
Only, love, I tremble so.

Kiss me once, and leave me, dear;
Better loneliness than fear.

Fear hath torment. Love, away!
I'm afraid of you to-day.

PERFECTED

Fear hath torment! Hie thee, Fear
I am safe, for love is here.

Give me courage; I am weak,
Darling, till I hear you speak.

Do I love you worthily?
Look into my eyes and see.

Do I love you very well?
Ask my heart, and it shall tell.

As the tempest rageth by,
Cling we closer, you and I.

In your arms and on your breast,
Though the worlds pass, I am blest.

Fear hath torment! Hie thee, Fear!
Love's security is here.

NOT YE WHO GOAD

Not ye who goad, but ye who lead,
    My laggard will shall move;
I know no right but equity,
    No road to it but love.

Love fits the precept to the need,
    Exacts of each its best,
Expects no lilies of the rose,
    Howe'er her heart be pressed.

The human whole is many-lived,
   Each life so set alone,
That who would win the world to tune
   Must love them one by one.

There is a clear truth knowledge-won,
   'Tis fitness makes for life;
And equity is fitness felt,
   Life-warrant of our strife.

But ere you light on equity,—
   O ye of book and rule!
Your hearts must learn the A B C
   In sympathy's own school.

STANZAS

We are, because we can be:
   We live among the flowers,
Grow e'en as they of sunshine,
   And all-prevailing powers.

No strength of the For Ever
   Could make me sing to-day,
Nor hinder this my singing
   This very day of May.

A DISMISSAL

   Away with light!
There needs nor sun nor star
Where I and my love are;
   Away with light!
Go, stars, where lives are old!
Go, sun, where hearts are cold!
   We need no light.

   Away with sound!
My heart thy heart shall reach,
Shall utter and beseech
What never word may teach;
   Away with sound!
Go, speech, where hearts are numb,

Go, song, where souls are dumb,
For us let silence come;
   Away with sound!

  Away with time!
Hours are for those who stay
Far from their love away;
   Away with time!
Together thus alway,
We know nor night nor day,
   Away with time!
Snatch from his hoary brow
Our own eternal Now:
   Away with time!

  Away with space!
The universe is here,
All glorious and near
Where life is warm and dear;
   Away with space!
Through all immensity
One blessed thing for me
Alone has room to be;—
   My darling's face.

HOPE DEFERRED

I've closed my book of hope, love,
   And folded down the page;
I'll read no more therein, love,
   Until some quiet age
When paler dreams than these, love,
   My chastened heart engage.

I'm going far away, love,
   Where no vain wish may thrive;
Where hope may lie quite still, love,
   Deep buried, yet alive!
And there I'll live alone, love,
   Till serer years arrive.

If then I should return, love,
   From yon forgotten strand,
And—your dear form all bent, love,—
   You greet me, hand to hand;
If then our eyes should meet, love,

I think you'll understand.

Q.—
Say, what is kindlier than snow,
   Warming the unborn flowers;
Or robin's little minor song
   In autumn's serest hours;
Say, where a gentler, tenderer thing
   In this harsh world of ours?

A.—
To make the best of chill To-day
   Earth snow of heaven doth borrow;
The robin sings of Yesterday,
   (Sing yesterday, sigh sorrow!);
But give me hope's own excellence
   Glad in her flawless Morrow.

The gentle vanishing of snow
   Ere yet the clod be broken;
The songless swallow's level flight,—
   Sweet summer's herald token;
The quiet greeting of true eyes
   Ere love's first word be spoken.

Sweet were the faiths our wishes bred; cruel is faithless fate;
All things show good or evil as we love them or we hate;
If what we love is what is not, our lives are desolate.

My faith had been in knowledge, and my watch-word had been truth,
My sword had been my courage, and my shield had been my youth;
But all had failed me now, hell yawned, and I was dumb for ruth.

Dead in their will-less shining; see the great stars there above
Hang where they can, and where the sum of chances lets them, move;
And being leads to living, and all living leads to love.

And round and round and round the sky the small world wandereth,
Best loving has mere issue in some re-beginning breath
That lives in turn, and loves in turn, and ebbs away to death.

'Twas poetry to sing it once, and half a cynic thought,
By way of momentary change from liege faith firmly wrought
Round a live God who made all life, and made no life for nought.

'Twas half a pleasure, then, to toy with half-imagined doubt,
And caustic just the tinge of pain that floated in and out
Among the vast, vague mysteries we felt and talked about.

Now, loving hangs on breath of life, and life on aggregates
Of motion, gathered into point and place in complex rates;
On what there is, on what has been, on deep compounded fates.

All through the tale of man the primal parable holds true,
The story of the fatal fruit at least is ever new;
Each deadly ill that came to us, came by the things we knew.

Choose we the blind obedient path of dull security
That smiles Amen to shibboleths it has no wit to see,—
Then, peace of moral fruitlessness, and will's nonentity.

Or rather, feel for certainty, and learn of good through ill,
And purchase joy by risking woe, change safety for a will,—
There dawns a truth, there sets a faith, there mocks mute heaven still.

Oh, what is it? What causes, and what issues from this thing,
Our piteous, grieving upwardness,—this hungry suffering,—
This worshipping of truth that pays our homage with a sting?

Thou, Man, in saddest wisest men, say, hast thou found thy goal?
Thou knowest of thyself at last,—thy tender body-soul,
Thine origin, thy deathwardness, thy fine-drawn fruitless whole.

Thy loneliness, thy lovingness, thy ceaseless, deepening care,
Thy slow, hot tears, thy worn-out faiths, thy choked, unuttered prayer,
Thy sickened hope, thy fettered will, and uttermost despair.

'Tis knowing that has brought thee this; thine honest search for light,
Faith yielded to thine earnestness, fate ne'er opposed thy right,
So gods and ghosts just flickered out, and left thee Fact and Night.

'Tis said—'No ill is absolute.' Yet, surely, pain is pain;
However sweet succeeding joy, no loss is ever gain;
Whate'er it lead to, weariness just is and must be vain.

See! everywhere and everyhow ill waits on wisdom's tact!
See! all our choice just lies between good fiction and bad fact;
Dares there a prophet hinder that I lie in thought and act?

If ignorance be bliss of faith, 'tis madness to be wise;
If seeing end in blinding me, 'tis well to close my eyes;
If life be dear, and truth be death, 'tis well to foster lies.

If life be dear! There hovers mute the grimmest question hree;
Ay, truly we are all undone if life be no more dear;
Here hangs our very final hope, our most tremendous fear.

For hourly more and more of fact is called upon by life,
And hourly yield the elements with less and less of strife
Such fit conditions as shall make the world with sentience rife.

And life will know and find its way in thought and word and will,
And life will grind and grovel on, will strain and struggle still,
Till knowledge of its powers' end its purpose shall fulfil.

More life, more knowledge every day, with less and less of mirth,
Now foot to tread old ways of pain on old tear sodden earth,
Is life so dear? Since now we know,—what know we of its worth?

Build up the faith in fantasy thou knowest thou dost need,
And pile beside it grief by grief the truths that make thee bleed,
So find the force and feebleness of that desired creed.

Liberty; loving; certainty; eternal room to be,
To live and love and work some work, effectual and free,
E'en in some great Companionship that loves thy life and thee.

This thy desire: beside it, just the rolling of the spheres,
The infinite unanswer to thy soul-deep hopes and fears,
The sinking of thy race and thee through merest lapse of years.

Truly if this be knowledge, then thrice blessed, ignorance!
Truly, if learning this for truth be meed of life's advance
The soul of man has lived too long, and overpast its chance.

Three prophets came to me at night when I was in my sleep,
They offered me, each prophet one, a purpose-clue to keep;—
For I was plagued to choose a faith amid despair so deep.

My knowledge had but mocked me when I tasted its ripe fruit,
And youth had chilled, and courage sickened to the vital root,
And truth had played me very false, and faith was numb and mute.

The first of those three prophets stood exceeding sure and strong,
I could have half believed his smile but that his voice was young,
He offered Life as faith of life, and so I knew him wrong.

The second of the prophets claimed omnipotence for Love;
He bade me help the flowers grow, and human hearts to move,
He called on all the universe his faith's firm ground to prove.

Aha! I knew the end of love; nay, worse, its origin;
The shiftless, sorry accident that things had stumbled in;—
Strong noose of fate that holds all souls to life, despair, and sin.

And then the pale third prophet spoke his quiet shibboleth,
He showed me how despairing ceased with ceasing of the breath;
I, living, could not know him false; and so I chose me—Death.

To be, is to be fettered; and all good is liberty,
I only shall be unenslaved when I shall cease to be,
I chose my deathward way;—the clue that leadeth to the free.

To make death swift and beautiful, to fill the world with death
That is pure death,—mere griefless ceasing of the toil of breath;—
The stilling of all strife in peace while old earth wandereth;—

To do this loyally is worth: yet still the task is stern,
My very soul must live to do it; merit it, and earn,
Till all the death-pain be burnt out a soul has skill to burn

Ah! seeking gentle death for all, I strangely found instead
I had awakened life that loved to live, and grief had fled;
Of all I touched, lo! nothing but the pain of life was dead.

I turned me to my prophets: were there three? or is there one?
A single spirit seemed to stand—Life, Love, or Death?—alone.
"Whom have I served of three?" I asked, in all perplexèd tone.

"Serve which thou wilt thou servest right, so only thou be true;
And call thy goal Life, Love, or Death, thou hast the self-same clue
To guide thee where new hope is won, whate'er thy heart may do."

And so I woke, and spread my helpless hands to heaven, and cried,
"Be this my dreaming true, and I will yield all joy beside,
If only, O Eternal, our despair may soon have died."

THE UNPARDONABLE SIN

I speak to women—woman I;
  I speak to one more heart beside;
  Whatever sin may e'er betide,

But one sin damneth utterly.

If you are pledged to love a soul
    By every pledge of love and law,
    But all too late you find a flaw
That bids your heart annul the whole;—

If hold to him you never can,
    Low as you are and all untrue,
    E'en this may be forgiven you;
You sin against a son of man.

But if, or pledged or free of troth
    (It matters not to savoured salt),
    If passion, pride, or any fault
Plead on the side of bliss for both;—

If when your will is evil most
    He strive to hold you to the right,
    If then you turn from him in spite,
You sin against a holy ghost.

Be very far this sin from me,
    Dear saint, whom I have loved so well;
    'Twould be the very hell of hell
To fail you for your sanctity.

HATED

You ask me where love fails me?—what I hate?
I cannot blame, for all, I hold, is fate;
Yet there are hateful, unblameworthy things
That sap life's nobler mercies at their springs;—
All deathward, pious-voiced uncleannesses;
All cold, conceited, mouthing meannesses.
Time-serving pietists who lie for fame
Sooner than hear no echo of their name;
Souls readier to limit all we hallow
By their own shallow thoughts, than deem these shallow.
Perfidious power that no compunction knows;
'Cute cleverness that makes convenient shows;
The devil-hearted insolence of sin
That to its end through broken faith doth win;
False woman who will fawn upon the neck
Of wife whose hearth she warms her by to wreck;
Some sneaking lover who for alien lust

Will mock his home and soil his social trust;
 The sour, uncandid treasurer of offence,
Who sneers down generous gift with common sense;
All cold, conceited, mouthing meannesses,
All deathward, decent-garbed uncleannesses;—
These and the like keep very far from me,
For all are lies, and all unsympathy.
Love cannot move them though it suffocate,
I do not blame—I absolutely hate;
Such things of folly, perfidy, and fiction
Must be; but they shall have my malediction.

"LET THERE BE LIGHT"

 Half prayed, and half commanded—Let there be light!
Light, where waits one undaunted, Blind with fight;
Light, where the lion-hearted, Lies in night.

 Light from due pain's red furnace, Light of love's sight,
Blend rays—O fierce! O tender! Lead him aright;
Shine for the just defender, The loyal knight.

 Where hope is yet the youngest, Let there be light;
Where grief has lain the longest, Let there be light;
Where will is still the strongest, Let there be light.

THE LIFE-POWER

 'Tis the marvel of existence,
    This great patience feeding things,
Till at last in myriad ages
    Wakes there one who sees and sings.

 Through the rifts of tottering temples
    Shines illimitable day;
Men begin to lisp its meaning,—
    Self must melt in love away.

 Never was the green of spring-time
    Half so beautiful to me
As when I beheld it growing
    Out of deep necessity.

 A necessity that sightless

More than sees the world it makes,
Ay, and more than knows the gladness
   Sinless life in living takes.

 Name it how you can and care to,
Words are vain and language rent,
'Tis too grandly simple for you!—
   Infinitely innocent.

HOW DO I KNOW?

How do I know you good?—my dear, my dear,
How do I know?
Because, at thought of you the bonds fall off
That plagued me so;
Because for love of you my very life
Has changed its flow.

 How do I know you good? Because, dear love,
In needing you,
My inmost soul most urgently desires
Great goodness too;
Pure skies alone can win a turbid sea
To perfect blue.

 One little lovely victory for your sake
O'er my mad blood,
One little hour when higher than myself
I knew I stood,
One stillness, dear, has taught the blessed truth,
My love is good.

 'Tis so I know you good—my dear, my dear;
My heart is new;
For your sweet sake 'tis less than virtue now
To be quite true;
Ay! easy to be patient, pure, and brave,
Quite good—for you.

STANZA

The sweetest song that a poet sings.
Though to your dull ear it be speech with wings,
He, singing, hears with a pent distress,

'Tis a cypher that stands for his speechlessness.

MY LITTLE TASK

I throw a guess out here or there,
I breathe a hope into the air,
I feel a dumbness like a prayer.

What, with this fencèd human mind,
What can I do to help my kind?
I such a stammerer, they so blind!

Nothing; save through the single gate
Of utterance throw my little weight
To swell the praise of what is great.

Nothing; save in my every song
Heap cold discredit on the wrong,
And cheer the march of right along.

And when I hear the lark's pure mirth,
Or see sweet flowers gladden earth,
Sing forth the mood that feels their worth.

Or when a bitter woe in me
Is healed by tender sympathy,
To let the healing songful be.

So add what force a singer may,
To ring opinion's echoing sway
A few chords mellower day by day.

Through chiming all that's pure and true,
Through hymning steadfast love anew,
This is the most that I may do.

"MERLE WOOD"

Dear, winding glens of Merle Wood! deep in flowers,
That speak the mood of peaceful, patient hours,
When human tenderness for nature's way
Coaxed her to richer sweetness day by day,
When gentle craft of philosophic mind
Luring forth beauty that it longed to find,

Here led leaf-tracery where rock was bare,
And helped a flower to light the shadow there;
Won from the woodland willingness new love,
And taught the grace of growing where to move.

Dear glades of Merle Wood! rich with clustered songs
Of little birds made welcome! healing trance
Visits my restlessness among you; wrongs
Vanish as spectres in the tolerance
Of nature's placid patience. Let me rest
Awhile 'mid proofs of lawful labour blest:
 These cool green haunts shut out life's weary dust,
And chide despondency: for lo! a trust,
Hidden yet perfect, where the calm thought bends
A bough to meet a future not yet seen,
Or buries seed where wilderness has been.
And honoured law in spring fruition lends
To bless the strong, sweet will whose means are nature's ends.

THE POET, AND HIS INTERPRETERS

Full of songs he woke one morning,
    Every song a weighty wonder
Holding universal being
    Newly dressed in words of thunder.

"Men shall hear me; men shall listen
    Through my song-speech sweetly seeing,
All the growing glory glisten
    Spread abroad in boundless being.

Spread yet centred, knit yet flowing,
    Constancy in revolution:
Still yet deathless; gliding, growing,
    And its new name—Evolution.

'Tis because the truth is tortured,
    Tinged by times and moods and manners,
Men reject the life of living,
    Write large lies upon their banners;

And with hearts all mad with yearning
    For a good they know not missing,
The inspiring essence spurning,
    Toil and die without possessing.

I will bring them truth ungarbled,
   Strike aside distorting lenses,
Methods, morals, metaphysics,
   Things and thoughts, and souls and senses.

I will show a mighty oneness,
   Every life-law underlying,
Make as nought the tyrant idols,
   Give men hope for living, dying.

What can cure their mad emotion,
   Yet not kill it in the curing?
How the voice of pain be silenced,
   While the voice of joy enduring?

What can wrench the sting from living
   With a knowledge of a dying?
What avail the heat of question
   If there never come replying?

What?—until the roots of sadness,
   Pressed too hard of life, grow rotten;
Till in grander grown emotion
   Self die down and be forgotten.

I will make men's hearts grow eager
   In the cause of law's own essence,
They shall fall in love with nature
   With a passioned acquiescence.

Till there shall be but one sorrow
   That can set the soul a-sighing;
Ignorance of law, or error
   In its incomplete applying."

So the Poet set him thinking!
   He would let no present blind him
To the tending of the future:
   And he left a book behind him.

And the crowd went blindly onward,
   Loving, hating, asking, solving;
And the little planet bore them
   Through the days and nights revolving.

While the poem of the Poet
   Waited praise that none would render;
Raised the bitter smile of cynic,

Set pain throbbing through the tender.

Till a little girl of twenty,
    Full of reverence for sages,
Found the book and called her lover,
    And they cut the yellow pages.

And they found a gem within it
    In the musical May weather,
With their young hands intertwining
    And their young cheeks pressed together.

For with loving hearts made gentle
    They divined a holy meaning:
Not in vain the Poet's sowing
    Since these joyed so in the gleaning.

Where the page was blank and yellow,
    Of love's own untaught providing,
There they read a text and moral
    That should serve their love for guiding.

And the Poet won his laurels
    Though so long his fame had tarried,
For they told their babies of him
    In the years when they were married.

LOVE AND LANGUAGE

Love that is alone with love
    Makes solitudes of throngs;
Then why not songs of silences,—
    Sweet silences of songs?

Parts need words: the perfect whole
    Is silent as the dead;
When I offered you my soul
    Heard you what I said?

AT SABBATH DAWN

Six times the sun has hotly lit
    A smoke-wreathed scene of care,
To-day the dust of toil is laid,

And children are at prayer.

Six times has tempest swept my soul,
  And now I gladly spend
A time of quietness with you,
  My patient, faithful friend.

There have been noons of warmer blaze,
  And midnights meteor-lit,
But never this most placid heaven,
  With heart-peace under it.

There have been throbs of stronger bliss,
  Yet is your presence best;
Safe in your firm and quiet hand
  My hasty pulses rest.

Too fiercely tides of life have flowed,
  And ebbed, alas! too fast,
Breathless and spent, I cast me down
  On tideless shores at last.

I do not ask if this be love,
  I know it to be rest;
The sabbath of my life has dawned,
  And I am very blest.

TELL ME

  Q.—
Tell me, Mother Nature, tell,—
What of heaven and what of hell?
Who doth ill and who doth well?
Tell me, Mother Nature.

  A.—
Well is done where firmlier life
Cometh forth from any strife;
Where life-happiness is rife:—
Love to live, my creature.

  Q.—
What of love? With what intent
Is my life with loving blent,—
Sacrifice and sacrament?
Tell me, Mother Nature.

A.—

Loveless life is null and vain;
Love alone is worthy gain,
Love alone is worthy pain;—
Live to love, my creature.

WHY?

A sweet white flower peeped
    Up from a glade,
Laughingly tossed its bell
    To the breeze that played,
Shrinkingly drooped and fell;—
    Why did it fade?

The river rolled; a beam
    Just glanced aside,
Making a thousand gems
    As it touched the tide;
Hid in a darkling cloud;—
    Why did it hide?

A mother watched her child
    At play hard by,
Dreamt his fair future through
    So lovingly,
At nightfall saw him die:—
Oh! why? Oh! why?

Tell me why sunshine pales
    And disappears?
Why are there faded flowers
    And mothers' tears?
Why are there babies' graves?
    And wasted years?

One who hath spelt his way
    To some great thought,
Through many a cloudy day
    And fight hard fought,—
One who has learnt the law,
    For ever one,
That tunes the children's mirth
    And lights the sun,—
One with a purpose pure

          As summer sky,
Whose human will with fate
     Makes harmony,—
One who hath skill to scan
The sole vast-hearted plan
That blends all men in man,—
     May whisper why.

MEASUREMENTS

Our world is very little in the sky,
     Far off she must be just a mote to see;
     And on the tiny ball creep tinier we,
To live a very little while, and die.

 My love is very great within my heart;
     It sees in two dear eyes, infinity,
     It finds in one sweet hour, eternity,
It has one measure:—nearness, or apart.

 Ah, well! both things are true as truth can be!
     The world is little and my love is great;
     Yet who would rise triumphant over fate
Earth's breadth, love's narrowness, must learn to see.

RELIGION

AN ESSAY IN COUPLETS

     What blesses yet is difficult,
This—goodness: worship, the result.
     What man doth worship man doth love,
And what he loveth he would prove.
     And if proof fail he'll place it high,
And claim a god's authority.
     What man can pray for, man can share,
His boon foreshadowed in his prayer.
     Were man of all his needs bereft
There would not be a bible left.
     Were needy man to lose his creed
To-morrow one would spring at need.
     Because men are by life enticed
They love their murdered Jesus Christ.
     Because their god is still their good,

Kind Christ was God in flesh and blood.
    Because they feel the hurt of sin
His mother was a maiden clean.
    Because men long for purity
He, born of her security.
    Because so many women fail
Therefore his Magdalen was frail.
    Because lone women need to love,
One Christ was set all change above.
    Some heart whose will could weakness be
Invented his Gethsemane;
    Some soul in passion's sore distress
Temptation in the wilderness.
    Since notions are not deep as needs,
Religion deeper is than creeds.
    If e'er the Christ be quite forgot,
'Twill be that love is needed not!
    Or else that love has found a way
To every heart of every day.
    The very truth is set at nought
If there be nothing lovely taught;
    And any solemn lie will do,
So it be sweet and solemn too.
    In all of which 'tis clear to scan,
Religion bindeth social man.
    What blesses, yet is difficult,
This—goodness: worship—the result.

THROUGH

A VISION OF VICTORY

I

Lo! one whose back was sunward, caught the eye
Of one who faced some horror in the sky.

With panic sickened and with deathly dread,
"What seest thou? in God's name!" he stammerèd.

Then from the drawn lips of that seeing one,
Hoarsely and low, "Look at that awful sun."

So, scarcely daring, half he turned, and saw;
And knew all Being changed into a Flaw.

Some say these two had sinned; maybe 'tis true;
Yet others say 'twas only that they knew.

Some say, "Black souls can e'en destroy the sun;"
Yet others, "Light too deeply may be won."

Who will, can hear; who can, will understand;
This truth may save his hope, and arm his hand.

Two things are evil in the universe—
Perfidy, and unpity. These I curse.

All else, not sin, but rebel incident
Good faith and pity live to circumvent.

II

Upon the middle plain of human life,
And at the middle hour of human noon,
The sun went black in the high midmost heaven,
And let the red up from the pit of hell
As beacon for the wandering of men.
And some there were who staid apart and died,
Rather than walk by luridness of glare;
These all were innocent. And some made mock,
And took to them young laughter and old lusts
And plunged into the glare; because that dark
Frightened them on the earth, and the new chill
Of God's extinguished noontide nipped their hearts.
And some of these were very glad of hell;
And some were sadder than all words can tell.
Yet Good and Evil sat, unmoved of all,
Each reigning o'er its band of following souls
Not by one soul diminished. But for hope,
It dived in hell-deeps; and, men said, there died.

III

Go to, fair spirits! checked and startled still
At oft-heard names of ne'er-imagined ill;
Go to, strong youth! white-hearted, eager-eyed;
Good faith, sweet pity, spare you for a tide.
Deafen your ears, enthusiastic lads!
Turn hence with veilèd faces, trusting maids!
Go, sift you by your soul-needs, and return,
As destiny shall drive you, here to learn.

Yet gather hither, souls whose brave despair
Refrains no less from perfidy than prayer,
Oh, haggard spirits of thought's storm-worn crew!
Would I might haven all your barks for you.
Pause in your wailings, poets of the night,
Pause in your revels, seekers of delight,—
Ye in imagination, ye in act,
Who face the fury, drink the dregs of fact,—
While I whose breath is passing, strive to tell
Of day-streaks shining through the floor of hell.
Heaven is o'erclouded. Yet the nether pit
Is wholly sounded: some have proof of it;
 Lo, one went down to see, whose witnes is
For all its depth, hell is not bottomless.
Chinks at the fiend's own feet let through a light
For eyes to see that weeping has made bright;
The night of sin has reached its blackest noon,
And there are dawn-rays that shall widen soon,
First for the poet- and the prophet-band,
Who past through fire to find them; then for all
Who, hearkening, have the skill to understand,
And bravery to answer the call.

IV

    A soul had speech with Satan on his throne,—
A soul that knew of pride and lust and rage,
And all the book of error page by page,
And all the sorrow that to man is known.
It had upon its forehead as it went
One star that lit its uttermost descent,
Kindled at that dead sun once long before,
Yet, source-forgotten, alight for evermore.
The star, some mere sincerity, at best;—
"Conscience" men call it;—and upon its breast
There blew a frail, sweet flower that did not die,
When depth by depth the soul plunged recklessly;
Some little blossom of mere tenderness;—
 Men call it "Pity" and its fragrance bless.
Satan looked covetously on these twain,
Twin passports through the region of his reign;
He sat enthronèd on that horrid floor
That let thin day-streaks through as through a door,
He might not pass the level of his throne,
To find the new hope that is love's alone;—
Yet thrice in stupid wisdom, lo! he sought
To filch the powers that set all sin at nought.

(Satan.)

"Yield me the star upon your forehead fair,
Yield me the flower you in your bosom bear,
So shall you soar again to earth and air."
    (Soul.)

"Nor gods nor men withhold the twain from thee;
But thine own recklessness of cruelty,
And thine own impotence of perfidy."
    (Satan.)

"Give them, and prove thy proverb by the test;
Give them, those trivial charms of brow and breast,
So shalt thou lightly mount to noonlight blest."
    (Soul.)

"Nay! though to lose them gave me back the sun,
So were the light of heaven too dearly won;
Nor heaven nor hell shall see my heart undone."
    (Satan.)

"Hist! Hug your fetters? fancies of an hour?
Your star of conscience and your pity's flower
Yielded, shall free your choice, and fit your power."
    (Soul.)

Nay; as a free soul came I into hell,
Not as a bond soul will I go from hence;
These which have passed me scathless as I fell
Will pass me further with their sweet defence;
Will pass me onward into depths of blue,
Where blooms again fair life for conscience true,
And heart that knoweth mercy. Down through hell
Behold me driven as prophet; thence to tell
That, deeper than its depths, all, all is well.

V

But, turning from the king of all despair,
The searching soul beheld a cynic there;
A poor, dejected, clever, mocking thing,
Half genius, and half sinner, and all woe.
Who set the very hell-walls shivering,
He scoffed and hated and desponded so.
The thick earth-sighs had filled his dulling ear,
Remorse had gathered in an unshed tear,

And such fierce drop had dried upon his eyes
That glittered with hard scorn toward the skies,
Till all his love grew recklessness of hate,
And all his thought, stark, bald, and desolate.
And as the soul of search went by, he sang
Till gruesome echoes rang:—
    "I laugh to hear you grieving, At the clearness of your ken,
At the loss of your believing, O on earth ye million men!
On the altar of your knowledge, On the altar of your truth,
Ye have laid your god, and slain him, In your strength of faithful youth.
What! ye loved him, and could lose him? Break your hearts to make him die?
What! ye held it ill to use him, As the crown of virtue's lie?
Nay, if this his use were evil, Brothers! brothers! what were good?
 There shall stand grim truth among you, Where your lovely lying stood.
Ha! my brothers, ha! my brothers, Will ye learn, who once forebore?
Then your souls shall grin and shrivel, As mine own for evermore.
Truth is not the deepest whisper, There is fact more deep than truth,
A strong thing, and a cold thing, Making silent mock at youth;
A clear, keen fact, confusing, All your good and ill forsooth.
Ah! I view the coils about you, Of a deep, denied despair,
Ah! I see the crowds without you, Turn and win them peace In prayer;
And I'll show you what you're feeling, Though your word be never there:
There's an order for the dying, There's a precept in the pall,
Yet there's bliss on bliss for living, Though the snake be in it all:
So saith silence when your hunger, Stares your conscience in the face;
So saith silence when your passion, Elbows thought to give it place.
Do ye wonder, shy and wistful, Lest e'en virtue's plea must die?
Do ye find no prize for seeking If on earth no sanctuary?
Ha! I cannot help you, brothers! Life lies open to the core,
And bawls its cynic secret, Brazen-tongued at my heart's door;
And True from Good I swear to you, Is severed evermore."

VI

    His head was up, his accent bitter clear,
There wandered by the soul of hope to hear
As he sent forth his cry, and broke anon
Its horrent deathliness of monotone
With cadence yet more hateful. None can tell
How drearier than all woes that ere befell
It is to laugh the shocking laugh of hell!
Whereat the soul of search looked straight at him,
So straight the brow-star grew a moment dim
At meeting, ray for ray, the chilly glare
Of soul-putrescence,—immanent despair.
 One moment; then resplendent shone the star,
And lit the hell-hole softly, near and far;

While from the fadeless flower such perfume went,
The foul pit seemed frank, fresh, and innocent.

   "O cynic! all whose lie is half a truth!
O cynic! all whose lying is for ruth!
For truth, and ruth, must I draw near to thee;
For truth, and ruth, do thou give heed to me.
Lie not, by all thy sorrow! Lo, the same
Thy quest and mine, which, each pursuing, we came
Here where no ill lies lower, and no shame.
Yet hast thou lost account of what thou art,
And needest one to show to thee thine heart;
A bud is pining on thy bosom now,
A weak star flickers palely on thy brow;
Thy hard tear is a tear because of ruth,
Hard and unshed it is because of truth;
See in mine eyes thy star reflected clear!
See how yon bud bespeaks thy loosened tear
To nourish forth its fragrant petals! Here,
O cynic, is my witness! Not alone
Art thou in hell—in knowledge. I have known."

VII

   Hell's very echoes dared not mock that tone,
But threw it back right gently—"known—have known":—
 A soul writhed in the saving, while there fell
Wavering and failing through the deep of hell,
"Known," "not alone," and "known." When echo slept
Hell was no more; for oh! the cynic wept.
The poisonous floor sank viewlessly away;
Being's round concave,—filled all full of day,
Mysterious, and ineffable, and fair,—
Sphered as a centre that delivered pair.
These watched the dawn-light widen for a space,
Each with glad love-tears shining on the face,
Then hand in hand passed forth to make essay
In the frank, virgin paths of life's new way,
Where purgèd souls renew a wiser youth
In the great daytime of love's stainless truth.

SONNETS

"WITHOUT REGRET"

Oh, when have after-days or evenings brought
   Forgiveness home to penitence downcast?
   Oh, when has trust been perfect,—honour fast,—
But fault or fate have made it all of nought?
What joy of ours is tinged not with a thought
   Of future emptiness, or wasted past?—
   What sorrow ever seems to be the last?—
What treasure found compares with treasure sought?

 In pale fruition we shall ne'er forget
   The splendid dream our eagerness did make;
   A shadow lies on all things;—let us take
Our share, and battle on a little yet.
   Friend, keep my hand! let friendship never break;
Let one thing be at least "without regret."

LOVE'S HEIGHT

Love's name is easy saying; yet who knows
   Love's uttermost, who loves not in his love
   The highest he has known, and yet above
That highest vision finds his idol grows?
Safe pinnacle of rapturous repose!
   And final agony of gladness! this—
   To spend thy conscience glowing in thy kiss,—
Thy soul's high best at one with passion's throes.

 No inward half-relentings, nought of rift
   'Twixt clay and spirit that should discord make;
   But awful, lavish homage, free to take
Only to give the richlier, gift on gift;
   No better self made captive for love's sake,
But love upraised to love, that love doth lift.

LOVE'S DEPTH

Love's height is easy scaling; skies allure;
   Who feels the day-warmth needs must find it fair;
   Strong eagles ride the lofty sunlit air,
Risking no rivals while their wings endure.
Yet is thy noblest still thy least secure,
   And failing thee—shall then thy love despair?
   Shall not thy heart more holily prepare
Some depth unfathomable,—perfect-pure?

Say that to thee there come love's dreadful call
    The downward swiftness of thy Best to see;
    Say that he sin or sicken, what of thee?
Are thine arms deeper yet to stay his fall?
    Scarcely love's utmost may in heaven be;
To hell it reacheth so 'tis love at all.

HER WORST AND BEST

O strange event of fortune that befell!
    She wandering, and you wandering,—each alone,—
    Met all amiss, and were asunder thrown;—
Two who were friends, and should have loved so well!
You knew the worst that in her heart might dwell;
    Her best the better flourishes unknown,
    Would rather win your welfare than be shown,—
Would give such gifts as least of giving tell.

So be it; go your ways: you were the first
    To wake stern aspiration in her breast
    For conquest, who had chiefly cried for rest,
And one pure draught of joy to slake her thirst;
    For this she owes her best-imagined best
To you, who found and spurned in her, her worst.

POOR LISA

Poor Lisa! Oft her folly has been sung,
    Of how she saw, and needs must love, a king,
    And make him know that wistful, tender thing—
Her little loyal heart—by minstrel tongue;
And how she felt herself more proudly blest
    Than many a bride, long wooed and triumphing,
    Who on her finger wears the plighted ring,
And lays her safe head on a husband's breast:—

Because her dear king hearkened to the bard,
    And royally came once to Lisa's cot
    And kissed her brow:—of how she deemed her lot
Rich at that hour beyond all dreamt reward!
    There the tale ends: it suits the singer not
To tell of Lisa's weeping afterward.

AM I TO LOSE YOU?

"Am I to lose you now?" The words were light;
    You spoke them, hardly seeking a reply,
    That day I bid you quietly "Good-bye,"
And sought to hide my soul away from sight.
The question echoed, dear, through many a night,—
    My question, not your own—most wistfully;
    "Am I to lose him?"—asked my heart of me;
"Am I to lose him now, and lose him quite?"

 And only you can tell me. Do you care
    That sometimes we in quietness should stand
    As fellow-solitudes, hand firm in hand,
And thought with thought and hope with hope compare?
What is your answer? Mine must ever be,
    "I greatly need your friendship: leave it me."

LOVE'S ETHIC

My love, despise not love in your high thought;
    For see what weakness finds the power to do
    Here in my failing heart for love of you,
And how my bruisèd, feeble hand hath brought
Here to your feet the treasure that you sought,
    Warm from the furnace of a passion true;
    'Twas perfect love made all my spirit new,
And helped me to accept the task you taught.

 Oh, doubt not! all the wisdom of the soul
    Grows wiser in love's light, and stronger still
    The sweet, fierce strength of high and holy will,
To be and bear and brave the very whole:—
    Ay, love doth aid the dauntless to fulfil;
And holds his compass steady to the pole.

YE POETS

Ye poets of our transient poverty!
    Weak strengths that pour sick passions into song!
    Who finding right struck dumb, enthrone a wrong,
And crown mean lust with love's own royalty!

Though I could find it in mine heart to be,—
    In some defiant moods at self's high tide,—
    A voice in your wild choir of craven pride,
Yet rather let me cease from minstrelsy
To grope for ever dumbly, onward still
Up the old rugged way, the blood-stained hill
That seen afar in youth seemed plainest road
Leading from self the slave, to man the god.
Yea, rather let me lay my music by
Than for mere music's sake hymn slavery.

TO A CRITIC

No theme for song—you say—the strength of man?
    Only his tyrant passion? Man, the slave,
    Fit theme for hymning? Never man, the brave,
Whose eye roves widely, clear as eagle-scan,
With vowed decision to fight out the plan
    Of mercy stedfastly, and sorrow save,—
Who taketh will for sword, and hope for stave,
And frowns down passion as a master can?

 Nay, give not whimpering lovers all the lays!
    Too long their tears have sodden soft your art,
    Till songs and sighs scarce know themselves apart,
And the sweet Easiest wins the proudest praise.
    Let music welcome some undaunted heart
That wrestles songless through the nights and days.

ONE MORE BRUISED HEART!

One more bruised heart laid bare! one victim more!
    One more wail heard! Oh, is there never end
    Of all these passionate agonies, that rend
Young hopes to tatters through enslavements sore?
So long, pale child, your patient spirit bore
    Its wrong in secret, ere you sought a friend;
    And yet, what love of mine can ever mend
Again for you the veil your tyrant tore?

 Oh, there are woes too bitter to be shown!
    Oh, there are tears too burning to be seen!
    Yet purest sympathy, select and clean,
May feel the agony its very own.

Sweet slave-child, whom your voiceless griefs oppress,
I cannot cure; I may in part express.

POET TO POET

Why on a day, half unawares and swift,
   Rent I the silence-veil 'twixt soul and soul?
   And flung down recklessly the very whole
Of all I was and am, for you to sift
The will-work of me out from passion-drift,
   And know my best and worst, and so enrol
   Me where I merit place 'tween start and goal;
In risk of trust, that justly you would lift
My meaning from my madness, shapely still,
   Not utterly dishevelled nor quite weak;
   Just one soul's voice the more, elect to speak,
Since having known the vale it chose the hill?
Why did I pour unbidden in your ear
The foolish tale?—Art's pride, in sooth, was here.

AT MY WORD

 I ever said that I could pay high toll
   For some dear sake held worthy, utterly;
   It was the very hidden pride of me
To rate as gift the greed of my poor soul.
For lo! one day I seemed to near my goal,
   And—"Here," I said, "my gift may given be,
   For here is utmost sweet nobility,
And I must love it: it shall have my whole."

 But, dear, such gift still savoured of my bliss,
   And you would have my love—for freedom—lie
   In sternest patience till its stress should die;
For love's last proof, forbear, forget the kiss,
   And smile, forgetting. Ay, I do not sigh!
Since this you will, my heart must grant you this!

DREAM-LOVE

I always seem to love you in my dreams
   Of force, and right, and nature, full and free;

Sleep after sleep, the very self of me
Lost in the nearest of your spirit seems.
Yet, as the grey of real daylight streams
   Across the bright deep of my passion's sea,
   There crawls a chill, a cloud up lingeringly
To sap the glow from night's divinest gleams.

 Which take for truth? Why are you ever twain?
   Awake, my intellect's serenest friend;
   Asleep, my being's sovereign, meaning, end,—
My heart's desire, delight, possession, pain?
   Ah! might I, dreaming, drive my love away,
   Or better, wake to find I love by day.

ONE NEW YEAR'S EVE

Heart! art thou dead within me? Why this calm
   To see thy joy die with the dying year?
   When more is fact than ever thou didst fear
Of all thou would'st not have of hurt and harm;
When less than thou hadst pictured is of balm
   In uttermost surrender; when more dear
   Seems that thou hast surrendered, now and here,
Than ever aught before? Why no alarm
To face the blank black morning of to-morrow
With not one partisan for thine own sorrow?
Why canst thou smile, O silly heart! to see
The cold strewn ruin of the life of thee?
Haply yet more than love's dear joy lies dead,—
Thy very self of self that sufferèd?

MAN VERSUS ASCETIC

(SIX SONNETS)

I

Soul, who would'st prove and know thyself for strong,
   Soul, who hast not a tyrant sin beside,
   Masked at thine elbow struts the flatterer—Pride,
Whose whisper has befooled thine heart for long.
Lash thee at thine own shrine with shameful thong?
   Soft-handed Nemesis between shall glide,
   To balk the smart thou seekest to abide,—

Daring at self's behest that holiest wrong.

Lo! thy good sword that seldom smites in vain
　　One day shall fail thy pride lest thou be lost;—
Slip in thine hold, and slay thine idol, Pain,
　　Win for thee treasure who would pay but cost;
Sweet punishment be pride's reward at length,
And thy best weakness save thee; not thy strength.

II

I mark thy clenchèd jaw, and murmured vow:
　　"Never—so help me Heaven!—will I be blest;
　　Never—so aid my will!—take any rest,
Nor common joy of lazier souls allow
My meritless endeavour. Rather, how
　　Most surely guard from recompense my quest
　　After the purely-high, mysterious Best;
And win it gladliest blood-sweat on my brow."

"O valiant to presumption!"—Nature cries,—
"This thraldom of self-will, I charge thee, break;
My children need thy bliss; and wilt thou take
At their discomfiture thy single prize?
　　Turn thee and dare be happy for their sake,
And smile up gratefully with childlike eyes."

III

"Peace with the vulgar counsel!"—dost thou say?—
　　Trumpet no mandates from the throne of sense!
　　Garb not as duty pleasant indolence!
Ever the loneliest is the manliest way.
Ever the flowers implore my hand to stay
　　And pluck their sweetness; ever some pretence
　　Slides to my soul, and mocks its impotence
Of ardour, with some taunt of faltering clay.

To fail, and only be as others be?—
　　All else I bear, all sorrow court but this!
　　Mine own soul's victory I may not miss;
And who but I can choose my pains for me?"—
　　Saith homely love, betwixt a sob and kiss,—
"'Tis I will find thy sacrifice for thee."

IV

"Nay"—yet again thou pleadest—"life is short;
  Lovers are many, heroes few and rare;
  Long years ago my one heart had its share
Of easy pleasure, and its evil wrought.
Leave me to my design, my single thought
  Just to grow perfect, inwardly aware
  Of victory than fairest bliss more fair;—
Shall my poor soul have freed herself for nought?"

"Thus much for thine own gladness. What for ours?"—
  Plead the unborn thy sons should live to aid;
  Pleads each most needy, noble thing unmade
That should reap heritage of thy won powers.
The Future pleads—"By all thy spirit can,
Be no mere saint for me, but loyal man."

V

Truly there is no nobler on the earth!
  Although such unemblazoned, simple lot
  Thy heart despiseth and believeth not,
Misdoubting man's good faith and woman's worth.
Here is thy sacrifice: no more to roam,
  Nor to seek out the soul's most barren spot
  To shrine thy will in; but, thyself forgot,
Spend all to found and fence one faithful home.

And see thy stark Ideal die in pain,
  And bear the throes it causeth thee to see;
  And quench the fires of lawlessness in thee—
For childhood's sake, endure a tender chain;
  Ay, on thy neck, in token thou art free,
Bear yoke of kinship e'en with lowlier men.

VI

"Ha! shall the living Needy miss my hand,
  Whom for my penitence I sought to bless,
  Till there depended on me numberless
Souls that unaided scarce have strength to stand?
Not only for my penance had I planned
  To succour these; I pitied their distress:
  Shall I betray them to their helplessness
For that new task? Is this thy sad demand?"

Oh, strength of tenderness! 'tis here I pause:
    I dare not answer; for to thee alone
    The weight and shaping of that claim is known;
Lo, even Nature has her minor laws!
    Yet fling thy will once down before her throne,—
Brave frankly her last verdict in the cause.

FOR FREEDOM'S SAKE

For freedom's sake, farewell. I would not fret you
    With a dim sense of bonds about your heart;
    Be freed of all my loving; let us part;
Let nothing chain your conscience, nor beset you.
A little while, may be, I must regret you;
    A little while—a little tender while
    Perchance the tears will well up when I smile
In whispering your name, ere I forget you.

 But we have chosen freedom; so I make
    Here,—as we part for weeks, for years, for life,—
    My promise: I will whet my will's keen knife
And one by one all memory's fetters break.
    Ah! go. Forget, forgive love's lingering strife!
One kiss?—our last. Goodbye,—"for freedom's sake."

www.ingramcontent.com/pod-product-compliance
Lightning Source LLC
Chambersburg PA
CBHW021942040426
42448CB00008B/1197